Everything Pure as Nothing

poems by

Patric Pepper

Finishing Line Press
Georgetown, Kentucky

Everything Pure as Nothing

*For My Wife,
Mary Ann Larkin*

Copyright © 2017 by Patric Pepper
ISBN 978-1-63534-353-3 First Edition
All rights reserved under International and Pan-American Copyright Conventions.
No part of this book may be reproduced in any manner whatsoever without written permission from the publisher, except in the case of brief quotations embodied in critical articles and reviews.

ACKNOWLEDGMENTS

Grateful acknowledgment is made here to the editors and staff of the journals where the following poems were first published, some in slightly different form.

BAP Quarterly (online), "The Big Snow"
Beltway Poetry Journal (online), "I'm Just Saying" and "Sleet, Snow, Cinders, Ash"
Districts Lines, Politics and Prose Anthology, Volume One, "It Snowed as in a Fairy Tale"
Innisfree Poetry Journal, "Father Nature"
Medicinal Purposes, "Proof" and "Driving in Snow"
Piedmont Literary Review, "Our Street" under the title "Perfect Snow"
Plainsongs Poetry Magazine, "Snow in Sheridan Circle"

Publisher: Leah Maines

Editor: Christen Kincaid

Cover Art: Nancy Whorf, *February Night*, PAAM Collection, Gift of Berta Walker, Courtesy of Provincetown Art Association and Museum (PAAM). Special thanks to Julia Whorf Kelly for copyright permission.

Author Photo: Mary Ann Larkin

Cover Design: Elizabeth Maines McCleavy

Printed in the USA on acid-free paper.
Order online: www.finishinglinepress.com
also available on amazon.com

>Author inquiries and mail orders:
>Finishing Line Press
>P. O. Box 1626
>Georgetown, Kentucky 40324
>U. S. A.

Table of Contents

One
Favorite Things ... 1
Shovel ... 3
It's Snowing in the Nation's Capital Again ... 4
The Last Snow ... 6
Late Lyric ... 7
Snow, Sleet, Cinders, Ash ... 8
Snow in Switzerland ... 9
I'm Just Saying ... 11
Fragment ... 12

Two
Snow Clouds ... 13
Father Nature ... 14
Snow in Sheridan Circle ... 17
It Snowed as in a Fairy Tale ... 18
Driving in Snow ... 19
After the Ice Storm ... 20
Snow, Just Snow ... 21
Proof ... 22

Three
The Big Snow ... 23
Cabin Fever ... 25
The Easy Storm ... 26
Rush Hour ... 27
Our Street ... 28
Our First Snow ... 29
Sure ... 30
It's Snowing in the Nation's Capital ... 31

Notes
Additional Acknowledgments

*Narcotics cannot still the Tooth
That nibbles at the soul—*
—*Emily Dickinson*

One

Favorite Things

It was 5:20 a.m. when I awoke to find I had
no reason to sleep except I needed the sleep,
but I looked out the bedroom window
and it was snowing, those tiny fluffy flakes,
a complete surprise, though only because
there was about an inch already, whereas
the weather forecasters said, "a dusting,"
and since this got me going I booted up
the tablet to find the forecast changed
to five to nine inches, so *Cool*, I thought,
and tapped on the YouTube app, searched
on "Coltrane," found "My Favorite Things,"
and then tapped on that as if I had a reason
to try to sleep some more, and listening
to Coltrane might put me out as I dreamed
about the sublime snow, but what I noticed
was Coltrane's version was so varied, so
sweet, so crazy, so cool, like an entire
amusement park full of distortion making
mirrors that catch us all exactly as we are
inside—*inside*, whatever that means—
and so I thought about the lyrics, snowflakes
sticking on noses and eyelashes, and how
his tonal chords followed by riffs, his pure
flights, how they provided exact counterpoint
for loveliness, so that he presents the whole
human being, like a plate of sweet and sour
pork, only profound in its nourishment, and
I knew then there would be no more sleep
that morning, as I had become too excited,
feeling that for that moment I had it all,

Coltrane's portrait of the real, my curious
notions, if only curious to me, and the snow
that would just keep snowing and snowing
as I played Coltrane's favorite things over
and over and over inside me, inside my head.

    2015

Shovel

Standing in the snow with my hands resting
on the grip of the shovel I remembered
Reed Whittemore, who could never remember
my name, and how he told me once in 1975
at the end of his 400 level creative writing class,
"This business has broken a lot of hearts."

But mostly I remembered the end of his poem
nominally about clamming with a bucket and rake,
"Son, when you clam, / Clam." I never forgot the pun.
Yet off I clambered over the jetties out to the flats
for clams, gabbing away in spite of his warning,
to get my heart broken, apparently never enough.

I shoveled on, ice an inch thick below the snow,
and 20 minutes later, stood, resting on the shovel
daydreaming, again, this time of Eugene O'Neill,
who continually shipwrecked his heart—even
when the gods were not shipwrecking it for him—
enough to win a Nobel Prize for writing about it.

His heart: He wrecked it, then raised it from the bottom
of the sea, knowing (not really) he had it in him
to raise it into the sun. So, the audience just sat
in silence, wept, not even clapping at the final curtain,
then crept to the stage to merely touch the actors:
March, Eldridge, Robards, Dillman, Ross.

O'Neill, he knew how to shovel, not just the crap,
but the snow, the snow, snow of the everlasting
fairy tales we tell ourselves. And then had the heart,
all bent and dented as it was, to hack away the ice
at the bottom of it all.
          My shoulders ached already, but
I dredged up Reed: Son, when you shovel, shovel.

2015

It's Snowing in the Nation's Capital Again

in mem. Leonard Nimoy, 1931–2015

Again. Third time in three weeks. Wow. It's snowing again.
One to three inches maybe. Schools opening two hours late.
I thought I heard a plow scrape by. "Jeez," I grumbled,
"more salt cracking up the pavement and ruining the snow,"

which the neighbor kids and I hope will paralyze the works:
Northeast, Southeast, Northwest, Southwest—everything.
I personally wish the snow would treat the government to a
meteorologically induced snowma: snow + coma = snowma.

The government would lie on life support under the snow
on the National Mall, dreaming of themselves caught on video,
and while the White House slept, the kids and I could build
a snowman on the South Lawn, charcoal for eyes and mouth,

archetypal carrot nose, an old pair of ear buds, and a sign
hanging around his neck that'd say: *Live long and prosper!*
When Congress, the Supreme Court, and the President awoke,
and the Mayor, City Council and District Attorney, too,

these foolish plows would be at last sold for scrap. And
everything would be "swell" again, as Granddad used to say,
snowma having whited out the Far Left and the Far Right—
hey, the Center: McConnell, Boehner, Reid, Pelosi, Obama,

who'd all have a bonfire, sled in Arlington Cemetery, then
hugging and weeping, would pass a great compromise:
kids *will* do chores *and* have the hot chocolate they need
and adults will be kindly *and* humble, or be fined $25 per

violation of this, The Empathy & Modesty Act of 2015.
Alas, I rolled over in the snow of my sheets and dreamt
of immigration reform, heavy weapons, Antarctica melting,
of the death of reason, meaning Mr. Spock and his salute.

When I awoke, again, I got out of bed, dressed in jeans, and a favorite old winter shirt going bald at the elbow, stood at my bedroom window, again, recalling other snow storms with their cold details. And I found my mind wistfully sane.

2015

The Last Snow

> *How can we certainly know*
> *If this is time*
> *Falling, or snow?*
> —Virginia Hamilton Adair

How improbable the forecast:
a fourth storm in four weeks,
snow so late this season, today
March 5, 2015, as if it were
still February, or even January,
not near the end and turning
soon to spring, with daylight
savings coming Sunday—
and seven inches. *Golly Neds,*
I think, as we used to say.
                    Not so
improbably, we're out of salt,
and the snow shovel is mangled
into scrap from chopping ice,
and the spade's cold steel has
grown dull and slightly rolled
at its point.
            Yet soon, fifty
degree weather will blow in;
nothing lasts forever, my love.
That's not even a clever thing
to say, and *how improbable*
isn't either, before we take
our nap this afternoon.
                    Yet these
are still eternal things to say,
meaning, forever-right-now.
So, I mention them,
            and I mean them,
as snowflakes fill up our street
so many years on from our
first snow,
    and we feel the heat, our body
warmth, again, along our length.

2015

Late Lyric

It started off
  as snow, mainly,
then turned to freezing
  rain, plainly.
I chopped the ice
  I couldn't persuade,
except to hack it with
  a long-handled spade.

I am very sore.
  Could I forego
such work I would,
  yet you should know,
I'm perfectly pleased
  it snowed.

2015

Sleet, Snow, Cinders, Ash

I heard it early pinging on the AC unit in the window,
as ambulance sirens—eternal, ever present, on the go—

rallied round our neighborhood in Northeast Washington,
en route to the scene of *WHAT?!*, where all deeds bad are done.

Then off to the Hospital Center a few blocks up the street
from our 1928-style-of-no-interest row house, replete

with all the poetry I can dream, read, steal, conjure, love,
mostly today this poem, which lacks a 21st century tough-

ness, describing how the pelting pellets turn to silent snow,
the way I'll someday turn to silent cinders and ash thrown

carelessly, on the Cape, behind our cottage, into the wind,
to get me that day into the marsh for which I'm destined,

as the wind transforms me into a storm of white, like snow—
there's the image: to be a bazillion flakes over North Truro.

2014

Snow in Switzerland

No snow all winter in D.C., though
plenty of rain, and we like rain,
the way it rinses the cars, the streets
and the gutters clean, how it dampens
the day into a nap day
and folds up life like an ironing board,
clankity-clanks it into the closet
in favor of minor daydreaming.

But we had no snow all winter,
albeit today, mid-April,
in a town called Schiers
beside the train tracks in Switzerland,
we awoke in a big brown house
that roosts itself on the side
of a towering wooded hill
and saw that it was snowing, easily,
all across the miniature valley
less than a mile wide.

We dallied over breakfast, which came
with our room. We sat and talked
with our host, Agnes, over muesli,
fruit and tea. The storm all the while
softly, softly in her big kitchen window,
with a little red train running the white valley,
as evergreens climbed the white mountain
on the other side. And though we dallied,
we finally managed to get out into the storm,
flakes the size of old silver dollars.

We watched, as toddlers might watch,
with aimless steps along the warm pavement,
where the fat flakes didn't entirely stick,
where they returned to plain rain. Watched
as they parachuted into Switzerland

to be our first snow, as we ourselves
poetized how we had parachuted
into Switzerland to see our first snow,
all of a grace, or luck, for winter had gone.

2013

I'm Just Saying

that if I had it to do all over again I'd be a meteorologist,
    not a TV weatherman, but a weather soldier deep
in the trenches of the National Weather Service, part of the
    anguish of big government the GOP might say, a noble
cog in a great wheel the Dems might say, though I might say
    that although I'm not happy and I'm not unhappy,
and though I'm definitely not both happy and unhappy either,
    anguish and nobility would lend to my forecasts sonority.

Anonymous in a beige fabric-covered cubicle with several
    computers tuned to satellites off in the cosmos, I'd fill
my screens with snow storms, pixels of our planet wearing,
    like an old aunt's downy curls, those pearly clouds that
highlight the blue, brown and green particle that is our home,
    on which we're chewing like termites chew a fallen tree,
though I would just comfort folks with scientific detachment,
    "Expect a dusting today; it is written all things must pass."

Over coffee, my boss would calmly grasp new radar patterns
    when she'd read my annual global reports. "Good work!"
she'd praise, darkening my cubicle door. She'd add my name,
    which'd be Walter. "Awesome, Walt, no snow jobs here."
She'd shoot me a wink, announce she'd like to send me off
    to teach in the "Clouds In The Classroom" program,
to show our students Power Point presentations of all types
    of clouds, knowledge to deepen and dignify their days.

Cirrus, stratus—ah, nimbostratus: They'd grin at the nebulosity
    of their small lives. Then, I'd return to my cubicle. I'm just
saying if I had a do-over I'd be a nondescript hero, a dull man
    who'd wear serious ties that change, daily, like the weather.

2012

Fragment

and when I came back to bed at 3 a.m.,
I whispered to you, and you to me,

—It's snowing.
—Is it covering the ground?
—No. It just started.
—It's not supposed to snow much.
—No. The flakes are small and slow, like vouchers.
—Like vouchers?
—Like vouchers.
—What do we get?
—Nothing.
—Nothing?
—Everything.
—Everything?
—Yeah . . . everything . . . and nothing.

c. 2012

Two

Snow Clouds

> *In snow thou comest—*
> *Thou shalt go with the resuming ground. . . .*
> *—Emily Dickinson*

Nothing so   leaden
so perfectly   pewter
so merely   monolithic
so deadpan   neuter

as just before   when
the flakes   descend

2010

Father Nature

> *Have you visited the storehouse of the snow*
> *or seen the arsenal where hail is stored,*
> *which I have kept ready for the day of calamity*
> *for war and for the hour of battle?*
> —Job 38: 19–23

Here's a little blow to sober you up   I do this for you   out
of universal compassion   but nonetheless for you   So
here we go   I come to you like an angel   in the form
you dig the most   in the form of   snow

I breathe over the planet   with a bit of weather   20 inches
in 20 hours   on top of the 24 you already have lying around
and as I breeze by   as you rhapsodize your poems in the
kitchen over a pot of tea   I give your house a bop on its noggin
as if to bellow   *Think Haiti.   Think Indonesia.*
Or better, *Think dead, your eyes—sockets filled with snow.*
         But I'll not crush, drown or otherwise kill you   today

You   hear your roof beam   *crack!*   then a smaller   *pop!*
then the big one   *CRACK!*   then watch a great maw in
your ceiling open wide as if to swallow—   *Me?*   You
mutter *Oh my god—*
                    and call the fire department
which arrives for your emergency   in their coats smelling of
smoke and boots leaving snow all over your Bokhara rug
and their classical helmets with little drifts of absolute snow
on the brims dripping onto their shoulders.

             The firemen   who check it out   in a hurry
to get to my next act of universal compassion   who tell you
         You have to get out of your house

         In a blizzard?   you wonder aloud

     The roof could go at any moment   the Captain states
             You can't stay in the house   and we
have to leave   and we can't leave until you leave
                 your house

The house you are fond of calling "the symbol of your soul"

You pack up a change of underwear   you stuff a partially-
eaten ham sandwich into your cardigan pocket   you help
your wife   as she helps you   to the sidewalk

                      where the snow still rushes down
      where you both watch the fire truck get stuck
in the 20 inches of snow   then dig itself out miraculously
wheeling off throwing snow wildly up under its fenders
you and your wife   chilling   there in the drifts before

        your soul with its broken skull

Soon you head over to Mabel's house   though you
have heard from another neighbor how Mabel heard her roof

   pop!   but just once   and it didn't come down

             While I   in the form of storm   keep
moving on   to the next act of universal compassion
compassion this time   though next time I may swallow you
   whole
                        And I never   and I didn't
   and I wouldn't   and I couldn't   put a thought in
your head that those who answer your prayer today are

                        Mabel, who took you in
out of the storm, and Nate and Jasmine and Jason who drove
you around in Jas's SUV, and Jane and James who fed you
and put you up, and Jean and Bob who opened their house
to you, and Heddy who most importantly pointed out how
things can go either way, and Rosario and Eber who shoveled
and swept and drove you home, and Stanislas the contractor
and Mr. Whitescarver the building inspector, and so on and
so on and so on for all the sixty years of your lucky life

And I   in the form of weather   the form of *whether or not*
pass slowly over the Chesapeake and the Delaware Bays
       as you call them   veer out over the Atlantic Ocean
           as you call it   and   "I"   in a swirl of
radar images
          I disappear

2010

Snow in Sheridan Circle

Each flitty flake a microscopic star.
Each a guest from Earth's own outer space.
Each a fragment of the unwriteable memoir.
Each a personage warmth will erase.

Together, they stretch across old Sheridan's arm
of bronze, and on Rienzi's flanks; they stick
to both like time itself, with all time's charm
cartoonizing them, right here in public.

Around the circle mute commuters poke
toward suburban homes: the great endeavor.
Snowy Sheridan would get the joke.
And the horse would be as noble as forever.

And I would be those flakes: playful, illiterate;
what a natty statue, maybe my favorite.

2007

It Snowed as in a Fairy Tale

> *Fairy snow, fairy snow,*
> *Blowing, blowing everywhere,*
> *Would that I*
> *Too, could fly*
> *Lightly, lightly through the air.*
> —Sara Teasdale

And we were giddy, knocking through the sideways,
    slanting, crazy-making snow,
fresh from the cautionary joy of WTOP radio,
as if we didn't know where we were walking—straight down
    Rhode Island Avenue NE
with the hiss and rattle of vehicles, the usual snafu
Washington becomes. We heard a whizzing Metro

pass above our heads, heard it whine to a stop. I
    looked up through the blow
of flakes at the very moment a very resolute freight train
    pushed past the growing traffic fiasco,
and then your boot kicked up a snow-entombed lump:
    a frozen sparrow, oh.
                  And still we were giddy.

Our boots: Our boots lumbered up 12th Street,
    left on Monroe.
We made the Shrine by two o'clock, that gigantic
    limestone curio,
authority in white one might easily misconstrue
but for the dinging of its bells inexplicably dinging then,
    as if the Shrine were dingy too.
Then Glenwood Cemetery—nearly home—the stones
    with jaunty hats of snow in a soft white meadow,
                  and we were giddy.

2007

Driving in Snow

So strong the pull of Heaven. I cruise along
at twenty miles per hour on a freeway
and watch the snowflakes fixing all that's wrong,
drawing the contours of one winter day
in simple white along retaining walls,
trees, power lines, everything, that's all,
as if a god's hot heart, in moody denial,
obscures the puzzling world with a little style.

Yes, I cruise bemused: I feel a heart—
or think I feel a heart—that's not unkind.
But I have to ask, *What have I in mind?*
His heart? Its heart? My heart? What is this heart,
right here, right now, all but invisible,
this slippery "Fact" about which I would scribble?

2005

After the Ice Storm

The ice has begun to thaw from the trees.
It drips and slips with a liquid ease,
according, it seems, to a natural vow,
along the cold, obedient boughs.

From the pavement its vapor rises.
The sun appears to force a crisis,
but isn't it truly vapor's role
to haunt the road like a supple soul?

The crows, to keep their boredom at bay,
are cocking their heads at this display
of ice and warmth—so water's ghost.
They mount their feathers and gently coast.

They ease along the hillsides of the air
as on licensed wings, as with genetic care,
adding with pointed clucks and caws
how they're in accord with nature's laws.

    'c. 2002

Snow, Just Snow

> *Snow is precipitation in the form of flakes*
> *of crystalline water ice that falls from clouds.*
> —*Wikipedia*

So, naturally one asks, "What is snow?"
A nuisance in Washington D.C.
A bliss in Washington D.C.
A menace at Valley Forge.
Nothing at all on Saint Lucia.
And recreation—did you know
there's a "ski resort" of sorts
on the Big Island of Hawaii?
Habitat for the Inuits.
Life and death for the Donner Party:

They became snowbound early, in late October,
in the Sierra Nevada, near Truckee Lake, where
they built tents and cabins, and then began to know
the economies of the Lord, when as companions
died, the survivors cannibalized the corpses—

Snow. A case of right or wrong?
Of good or evil? Or just a case of cold?

2001

Proof

> *Each particle an illusion; yet massing. . . .*
> —*Virginia Hamilton Adair*

Over the National Mall a surprise snow
incorporates itself by random pattern,
making of monuments a white tableau.
I stand. I watch. I breathe out clouds and yearn

in the regular irregularity
of the six pointed flakes that drop dreamily,
striking the earth as if they had a mission
to disinfect our town, and keep us wishing.

Aimlessly as they fall, see how they bring
order at last, building the perfect pile
neat and level, rising purely pale?
Surely it's cause for hope, and we should sing.

I feel these thoughts and long for bells to peel,
certain they wouldn't prove a blessed thing.

2001

Three

The Big Snow

    Everyone seemed giddy.
    The government shut down.
The storm was pouring it on the city,
    muffling every sound.

    Buxom with heavy tufts,
    the evergreens were bent.
They looked as if they'd had enough
    of fortune's quaint descent.

    The children were set free.
    Each one found a sled.
Down the slopes of a cemetery
    they screamed among the dead.

    The homeless bundled up,
    and slid their carts away.
Who knows to where they trundled off
    to watch the weathers play?

    While through the avenues
    the tire tracks were filling,
the work force gone to watch the news
    and cozy up that evening.

    Except for those who galoshed
    through city parks by chance,
who muttered to themselves, "My gosh,"
    and watched the snowflakes dance.

For tumbling fluff descended,
"Oh certainly choreographed,"
the flake ballet they dreamed again,
lightheaded, almost daft.

Made so by this visit
from the heavens to below
although, despite the fact, albeit,
it was only snow.

2000

Cabin Fever

Arrested by a foot of snow,
   we then atoned
   as like white loam
ice came to earth, settled below
   the sash and in the street.

Although the snow caused our retreat,
   we didn't brood;
   humbled, and nude,
we gloried in each other's heat
   and took ourselves to bed.

After every word was said,
   forgetting clever,
   we lived the fever;
flushed, we took the great instead,
   a nap with the *us* we love.

Soon, as if snow weren't enough
   to guard the door,
   we whispered more,
our happy dream complete, the proof
   of love, if just for *us*.

c. 2000

The Easy Storm

November snow, a light and lazy fall,
   each flake a colony of flakes meandering
down the ethers of this world. No pandering
   here to gods and demigods, no call
for time beyond this afternoon, as jays
   in dusty blue roost in a locust tree,
and crazy sparrows wrangle endlessly,
   bumbling about a yet-leafed weedy maze.

I was a flock of sparrows once—such raging heart,
   Cheep-cheep! Cheep-cheep! in beauty's hush—
or like one anyway. They hop and dart,
   but the blue jays, oddly silent, flush
at my approach, into the easy storm,
   content with self, its dusky feathered form.

1997

Rush Hour

    Miles from work a blinding snow
        maps the brittle air,
careening from clouds to the pavement below,
        down an invisible stair.

    We spin our tires, our tail lights glow
        to blaze a path somewhere.
Then, strangely, the *caw!* of a plummeting crow
        lightens our despair.

    How do you do, you swooping shadow?
        Why don't you just declare
how silly we are as away we don't go,
        mumbling, "It isn't fair."

    The motor grumbles. Next the radio
        gives us a real scare,
"Drive if you must! If you can, don't go!"
        The commuters creep and stare.

    1996

Our Street

A perfect storm: several inches
   that falls on Friday night.
Better than one that comes in pinches,
    or, kids' delight,
a blow that pounds a couple of feet.
    A treat
to watch it from our bedroom window,
   my arms around your waist:
the fall and rise, the coats of snow,
    the cars encased
until they look like loaves of bread.
    And dread,
of slipping down the upward street,
   never enters my head.

1995

Our First Snow

> *But you, like snow, like love, keep falling. . . .*
> —Robert Penn Warren

The harmony of these flakes
as fast they feather past
the matter-of-fact lamp
on the hush-sweetened street
is not for our sake,

even as I say, "Look,
how evenly spaced." And you,
"Doesn't your heart just break?"
As not even clever, we say it,
and mean it, "I love you—
    forever."

1992

Sure

> *When you understand one thing through*
> *and through, you understand everything.*
> —Shunryu Suzuki

Sure, I knew what snowflakes look like.
But today they crashed on the windshield as I
sat in my parked car in White Oak, Maryland,
and sure they fell from the sky, but also fell from
none of those National Geographic magazines,
children's books, and chemistry texts. They plunged
from the heavens. That's right, the heavens, and they
looked bizarre, like stars, like cookies, like maple
leaves, like pinwheels, like candies from another planet.
They looked like poetry itself, there for the reading.
And they rested like . . . forever, for a short while,
then did a quick shrivel into water, into sole seeping
sock soaking H_2O: water. Sure, I already knew what
snowflakes look like, but today I thought I understood.

c. 1980s

It's Snowing in the Nation's Capital

"The stars come down!"
you greet the snow.
In our southern town,
mass vertigo:

Washington wrapped in hush,
as odd is evened,
and white and lush,
all things are leavened.

We stamp our shoes
and linger here,
as if good news
has filled the ear

at last: everything,
pure as nothing.

National Mall, c. 1980s

Notes

Leonard Nimoy, 1931–2015, played the ultra-rational Vulcan, Mr. Spock, in the 1960s television series *Star Trek*. Mr. Spock often gave the "Vulcan salute" and said, "Live long and prosper." His death was announced the morning the poem "It's Snowing in the Nation's Capital Again" was written.

The poem "Favorite Things" alludes to John Coltrane, the tenor Saxophone player who recorded a now classic jazz version of the Rogers and Hammerstein song "My Favorite Things."

The play alluded to in "Shovel" is *Long Day's Journey Into Night*, in fact, a particular performance on Broadway in November of 1956, staring Florence Eldridge, Fredric March, Bradford Dillman, Jason Robards, Jr., and Katherine Ross, at the end of which the audience was said to have been so stunned that they didn't clap. Rather, they approached the stage to reach out to the actors with their hands.

Additional Acknowledgments

"Rush Hour" and "The Easy Storm" first appeared in *Zoned Industrial*, published by Poet to Poet, 2000; second edition published by Banty, 2010.

The epigraph for this chapbook is from Emily Dickinson's poem 501 [This World is not Conclusion,].
The epigraphs for "Proof" and "The Last Snow" are from Virginia Hamilton Adair's poem "White Darkness."
The epigraph for "Snow Clouds" is from Emily Dickinson's poem 1669 [In snow thou comest—].
The epigraph for "It Snowed as in a Fairy Tale" is from Sara Teasdale's poem "Snow Song."
The epigraph for "Our First Snow" is from Robert Penn Warren's poem "Love Recognized."
The epigraph for "Sure" is from *Zen Mind, Beginner's Mind*, by Shunryu Suzuki.
The poem "Shovel" quotes Reed Whittemore's famous poem, "Clamming."

Many thanks to the members of the Capitol Hill Poetry Group who from 1982 through 2015 read and critiqued these poems.

Many thanks to Jean Nordhaus, Anne Harding Woodworth and Greg McBride for taking the time to write comments for this chapbook.

Last but not least, special thanks to Mary Ann Larkin, Sid Gold and David Salner for reading this chapbook in manuscript. Their suggestions made this collection possible in its present form.

Patric Pepper is the author of two other collections of poetry, a chapbook, *Zoned Industrial*, Poet-to-Poet's 2000 *Medicinal Purposes* Chapbook Contest winner (Banty, expanded second edition, 2010), and a full-length collection, *Temporary Apprehensions*, winner of the 2004 Washington Writers' Publishing House Poetry Prize. From 2008 through 2013, Pepper was President of Washington Writers' Publishing House, a cooperative poetry and fiction press that began publishing in 1975 and has published well over 100 books to date. He continues to volunteer with WWPH, currently serving as Production Coordinator. His work has appeared in numerous journals and anthologies, including most recently *Beltway Poetry Quarterly, The Broadkill Review, Cape Cod Poetry Review, Confrontations, District Lines, Fugue, Gargoyle,* and *The Innisfree Poetry Journal*. With his wife, the poet Mary Ann Larkin, he is cofounder and publisher of Pond Road Press. A native Washingtonian, he lives in Northeast D.C. and North Truro, Massachusetts.

www.ingramcontent.com/pod-product-compliance
Lightning Source LLC
LaVergne TN
LVHW041553070426
835507LV00011B/1072